My Poetry Book

Filled with Love, Joy, Sadness, Happiness, and Motivation

Frances J. Hill, Ed. S.

Copyright © 2020 Frances J. Hill, Ed. S.
All rights reserved
First Edition

PAGE PUBLISHING, INC.
Conneaut Lake, PA

First originally published by Page Publishing 2020

ISBN 978-1-6624-2374-1 (pbk)
ISBN 978-1-6624-2375-8 (digital)

Printed in the United States of America

Joy

Joy is like flying,
Feeling the air beneath my wings,
Like a plane gliding through the sky,
As if there was flash of light
Streaking through the night.

Joy feels like lying on a pillow of cotton candy.
Joy is sweet and dandy,
Soft, fluffy, mushy, and puffy,
As smooth as a bowl filled with marshmallows,
Just like the sun, bright and yellow.

Joy is like being in a field with a host of golden daffodils.
It gives you a feeling like dancing in the breeze.
A Flag blowing with ease,
As though I had given it a big squeeze,
Full of blissfulness, blessedness, and gladness.

Joy, joy, and oh, joy!
As if dolphins were leaping and spinning like a toy
On a big ocean top.
My, what a pleasure you are!
Joy will leave no scar.

How beautiful is this joy?

Time

Time flies and flies.
It is here one minute and gone the next,
Like the twinkle of an eye,
A streak of lightning crossing the sky.
In a flash, it is out of sight.
It zooms by like a light
In the middle of the night.

Ants

So tiny and small
Yet so strong,
An insect with a complex
That works with a group,
Nevertheless, is capable of performing special duties:
The mighty ant.

Life

L is for "lilies."
I is for "innocent."
F is for "fullness."
E is for "everlasting."

So live life like a lily
In an innocent state
To the fullest and happiest everlasting
life!

My Ship

Most people say, "I'm going to wait until my ship comes in."
However, when that ship comes ashore,
They say, "I am going to wait for one more,"
Sitting by the waste side,
They wait and wait and wait.

Days come, and days go.
No ship would ever blow.
The ships kept rolling by,
As if to say, "I am here to spy."

So, stop waiting for the ship.
It is time to get off the bank.
Swim out to meet the plank,
My ship!

CLINT

C is for "cleanliness."
L is for "love."
I is for "impact."
N is for "never saying goodbye."
T is for "totally loved."

The cleanliness of love shows,
The more impact it has,
The more it leads to never forgetting.
Endless but totally loved
Forever and ever,
CLINT!

Reasons

There are reasons to cry,
Reasons to sing,
Reasons to eat,
Reasons to sleep,
Reasons to dance,
Reasons to laugh.
The best reason of all
is the reason to live!

Mountain

I am so high you cannot see over me
I am so wide you cannot see around me
I am so thick you cannot see through me
I am so deep you cannot see under me
However, I am so beautiful you cannot keep your eyes off me
I am the mountain

My Daddy

He is big
He is tall
He is bright
He is smart
He is handsome
He is loving
He is giving
He is graceful
Best of all, he is my daddy

Mother

Mothers are sweet
Mothers are kind
Mothers are always around
Mothers pick you up
Mothers lay you down
Mothers never let you down

My Love for You

You are my love today and forever
The elastic of my heart stretches around you
The tenderness of my arms lies upon your shoulder
The gentleness of my touch evolves deep within your veins
The softness of my voice rests in your ear

The desires of my heart keep growing each day
My love for you will never fade away
The dreams of night may never sway
You are in my heart to stay

If you decide to walk away
I am strong enough to let you stray
For I know one day
You will be back to stay

This Land

This land is wide
This land is beautiful
Full of trees and
Full of birds
Full of flowers and
Full of animals
Full of insects and
Full of reptiles
Full of mammals and
Full of fish
Full of colors
This land

Squirrels

Bushy tails
Gray and furry
Quick and fast
Medium or small rodents
Live in trees
And beneath the ground
Squirrels are neat to have around

My Country

My country is where the garden
Are grown by hands
Tractors clear the fields
Farm animals walk around the pasture
Neighbors are eager to lend a hand

Communities are considered as one
Families see about one another
The passersby wave their hands as
Grandparents sit on the porches
There are no strangers around

The children respect all adults and
Adults raised their children
The next-door friends disciplined
The neighborhood children
Love is spread throughout the town

This is my country

Eyes

Can eyes deceive?
Can eyes be trusted?
Can eyes see lies?
Can eyes see true love?
Can eyes lead you wrong?

Can eyes see fear?
Can eyes see pain?
Can eyes see hurt?
Can eyes see joy?
Can eyes see sorrow?

Can eyes see tomorrow?

Scared

Scared straight
Scared light
Scared up
Scared down
Scared right tonight

Bees

Bees can fly
Bees are small
Bees are insects
Bees make beehives
Bees can sting

Bees can pollinate
Bees produce beeswax
Bees can live underground
Bees can be around
Bees can live downtown

Bees can cost money
But best of all
Bees can make honey

The Lady of This House

This lady is strong
This lady is mighty
This lady is free
This lady is honest

This lady is sweet
This lady is neat
This lady is kind
This lady is helpful

This lady is caring
This lady is tender
This lady is a mother
This lady is a workaholic

Leaves

Falling to the ground
Turning brown, dry, and rusty
Blowing in the wind
Blowing through the air
Leaves are everywhere

Days

Days are bright and sunny, briskly as a summer morning
Breezes blowing through the trees
With the birds singing and chirping in the air
Like a room filled with angels
Singing to the highest of all

Days bring joy and happiness throughout the years
Days make the dark nights brighter
Days are our light to the tomorrow
Days challenge us to be better selves
Days are a way to help improve yesterdays

Days are meant for a new beginning
Days end the old situations and enlighten a new start
Days are our way to begin another course or journey
Days are wonderful an amazing
Days

Love

Love is unexplainable
Love is irresistible
Love is challenging

Love is irritating
Love is dictating
Love is an itching and tickling in your heart

Love is emotional
Love is affection
Love is devotional

Love is passion
Love is honest
Love is loyalty

Love is something you cannot scratch
Love is in your mind
Love is in your soul

Love can break your heart
Love can make you happy
Love is always sappy

Traveling

Traveling by cars
Along the highways
Over the mountains
And through the valleys
Where there are no alleys

Traveling by planes
Landing from strip to strip
Countries to countries
Continents to continents
Trying to avoid accidents

Traveling by ships
Pulling from docks to docks
Crossing the oceans
Crossing seas
Smelling the ocean's breeze

Traveling takes you on a world of adventures
Therefore, sit back, relax, and enjoy the ride
Traveling is the way to move your hide

Temptations

Temptations drive us in many ways
Encourage us to overcome obstacles
Give us the desires to take chances beyond the norm
Tempt us to run away and escape trouble
Urge us to do or not to do something
Whether it's good or bad
Right or wrong
Persuade one to perform acts for pleasures or gains
Temptations are inevitable

Tops

Round tops
Flat tops
Oval tops
Square tops
Long tops
Short tops
Tops cover every drop

Sunrise

Sitting on the porch, looking through the trees
Coming over the horizon
What an amazing sight to see
A bright and beautiful glow of
The sun appearing through the woods
Yellowish and orange colorings
Lighting up the sky
High rising and up rising
To an awesome and wonderful way
That makes a glorious day

Vacation

A long year of pondering,
Wondering, examining, thinking,
Planning, looking, searching,
Longing for this day—
Vacation.

It takes you places all over the world
From land to land, state to state,
Town to town, city to city,
Ocean to ocean, and sea to sea—
Vacation

A period of spending time away from home,
Scheduling, waiting, living in suspense
For that day of laughing, joking,
Dancing, and eating—
Vacation

A temporary time of rest and delays
From stress, paperwork, meetings,
Conventions, speeches, reports,
Workshops, and working—
What a vacation!

Birds

Blue birds,
Red birds,
Jaybirds
Fly high,
Fly low.
How far can they go?

Courage

It comes from within
Gives you the ability
To face pain and sorrow
Helps you tackle danger
Courage persuades you to venture out

Courage is bold, strong, fearless
Daring, powerful, and gutless
It makes you strong and mighty
Most of all, it provides you with the strength to endure challenges

My Brother

C is for "Christlike."
L is for "loyalty."
I is for "inspiration."
N is for "noble."
T is for "testimony."

Who has the Christlike love and loyalty *like* CLINT?
My brother.

Lady

Brown and white
With a heart of gold
Walks with a twist that is big and bold
My sweet lady

She runs and jumps high in the air
Like a deer rising and leaping over a fence
She has the speed of a gazelle as swift as lightning
She is my sweet lady

With her unique humanlike behavior
She loves to protect and aid others
Like a hunter, hunting is her thing
My sweet lady

She thrives with energy
Like a cheetah
Her coat is smooth and shiny
My sweet lady

Regrets

Regrets are things that have gone wrong
Things that never happened
Things that changed lives
Things that caused trouble
Things that caused problems

Regrets are things hated
Things done because of hatred
Things done in the name of love
Things done in the name of caring
Things done in the name of happiness

Regrets are things that cause families to fall apart
Things that cause loved ones to move far away
Things that cause friends no longer to get along
Things that cause divorces
Things that cause lives to be lost

Regrets cause one to do the wrong things for the right reasons
Regrets are sorrow felt deep inside
Regrets are hard to overcome
Regrets should never last long

Regrets, regrets, regrets

Family

They love and support you
Family chastises you when needed
Guides you in the right directions
Praises you after achievements

Family laughs with you in time of happiness
They cry with you in time of sadness
They build you up when you are down
They hold you in time of losses

Regardless of all the good things
Family tears you down
They break your heart
Put you in a bind

Family causes trouble
They also inflict pain
There is nothing like family

The Lantern

The light that guides you
Through the darkness
It lightens your pathway
It shows you the way

It brightens the night
It is a torch in outdoors
It is a signal for safety
It generates light to lead you home

The source of lightning
Leading you with a flicker
Of brightness as you travel
On your journey
The lantern

A Long Walk Home

As I walk alone wondering what I might see
Down the long and lonesome road
With nothing in sight
A slightly lit sky and woody forest

The sounds of crickets and critters of all kinds
The fresh air of sweet-smelling flowers and honeysuckles
The creepy crackling of the trees
The running of rushing brooks and streams

My mind is straying in many directions
Looking wide-eyed and spread nostrils
Ears stretched as far as they can go
As I walked the narrow the road

My fears grew and grew and grew
The pounding sound of heart got louder and louder
Hearing the frightened beating of my heart
I became terrific and panicky

My feet was moving as fast as they could go
Bounding the rough and rugged road
Afraid to look from side to side
Listening to every moving sound

Then all of a sudden, I saw a bright light
It was the light from my porch
Finally, I am home from a long walk

Listen

Are you listening?
Can you hear it?
The soothing, calming sound of music?
The relaxing, comforting
Harmony of words?

Are you listening?
Can you hear it?
The soft, sweet lingering
Sound of rain falling on the rooftop?

Are you listening?
Can you hear it?
The crackling of fire in the fireplace?
The whispering of the teakettle on the stove?

Are you listening?
Can you hear it?
The sparkling sound of pouring white wine?
The ice cubes clinking into the glass?

Are you listening?
Can you hear it?

The Last Dance

As we danced our last dance
The joy of seeing the smile on your face
The enormous sound of happiness in your voice
The smoothness of movements in your steps
I did not know it would be our last dance

The joy on the faces as they watched us
The applauds we got as we glided across the floor
The glow of the lights that shone upon us
The glistening of their eyes as they looked at us
I never knew it would be our last dance

The enthusiasm you had while singing
Prevailed the love and interest you had about life
The love that you showed me as we dance
That love will forever be in my eyes, heart, mind, and soul
I never knew it would our last dance
You saved the last dance for me

That Is What They Say

You cannot do that.
You cannot make it.
You cannot move away.
You cannot have that job.
That is what they say.

You cannot have that.
You cannot create anything.
You cannot sing.
You cannot dance.
That is what they say.

You cannot play sports well enough.
You cannot go college.
You cannot go pro.
You cannot become famous.
That is what they say.

You won't amount to anything.
You will always be the same.
You are just a troublemaker.
Nothing good will ever come of you.
That is what they say.

Question:
What do you say?

My Daughter Jamie

When you came into my life
You lit up my world
That big smile on your face was amazing
You are my daughter, Jamie

Daughter, you are my joy
You are as bright as the shining star
You light up the room with your beautiful laughter
You are my daughter, Jamie

The way you enter a room is breathtaking
The elegant way you move is inspiring
The impressive way you greet others
You are my daughter, Jamie

The way you help others is a blessing
You take the time to say hello
You never met a stranger
You are my daughter, Jamie

Don't Start Nothing, Won't Be Nothing

If you don't want it
Then don't start nothing
And it won't be nothing

If you can't handle it
Don't get in void
Then it won't be nothing

If you can't stand by it
Don't start nothing
It won't be nothing

If you don't believe in it
Then don't say it
Then don't expect nothing

That's My Child

He was bright and smart
Intelligent and loving
Tall, lean, and sharp
That's my child

He grew up and away
Withdrew from school and work
Left family and friends
Regardless, that's my child

He made bad and worst decisions
Lost his home and family
Lived on the street
Nevertheless, that's my child

He never asked for handouts
He moved from town to town
Criticized by neighbors and strangers
Yet and still, that's my child

Then one day, he was standing in the doorway
In one hand was his suitcase
The other hand was a certificate and diploma
I proudly said, "That's my child'

The Big Valley

A big open range with beautiful fields and trees
Where the air is fresh and clean
The horses run wild and free
The flowers grow tall and wide

A flat, low, and smooth region
As the streams flow through the valley
With cool rushing waters between the hills
A place where peace and quiet lie

A site formed by slopes and plains
That made the spaces between them
This great hollow range
Where the birds fly and deer eat and roam

The setting with fertile soil and excellent farmland
A spot allowing cows the luxury of grazing the open fields
A location where children can run through the meadows with ease
Where they breathe the air in breeze
The big valley

Star

You were like the star in the sky
Bright, clear, and shining beautifully
Lighting up the smiles on the faces you met
So vivid and blazing as you pass by
You were a shining star

The dazzling way you made others feel on a bad day
Once they saw the beam in your eyes
That canny look on your face
Just brightened their day after you said hello
Then you went on your way

You were a light in a bottle
A delight for other in every way
The radiance you gave off glowed in your pathway
The twinkle in your eyes made our day
You were a shining star

I Made It

I'd been misused and battered
Lied to and cheated on
Told I was not the one
However, I made it

My hopes and dreams destroyed
Laughed at and joked about
Oxidized and criticized
Nevertheless, I made it

Had broken promises
Been bruised and knocked down
Rejected and torn apart
Yes, I made it

Sent away by loved ones
Closed doors in my face
Denied promotes
Guess what, I made it

Regardless of the struggles
Regardless of the hard times
Regardless of the pains
Thank God, I made it

Today

Today I woke with a smile on my face
Today the birds were singing
Today the flowers were blooming
Today the sky was clear and bright

Today I learned I did not have a true friend
Today I learned that being alone is hard
Today was one of the worst days of my life
Today I had to learn to enjoy myself

Today I started a new chapter
Today I decided I would not look back
Today I broke the cycle of fear
Today my life became dear

Today I made a new beginning
Today was the first day of the rest of my life
Today I learned to live free
Today I learned to be me

Thank you, God, for today

Dreams

Dreams are things that make you think.
Dreams are looks into the future.
Dreams are warnings while you sleep.
Dreams prepare you for tomorrow.
Dreams, dreams, oh sweet dreams.

Dreams are not to be ignored.
Dreams are interpretations of what's to come.
Dreams help you to focus on truths.
Dreams of realizations of facts,
Dreams, dreams, oh sweet dreams.

Dreams come as a reminder of what you already know.
Dreams are our connections to reality.
Dreams carry us from darkness to the light.
Dreams help make things alright.
Dreams, dreams, oh sweet dreams.

How precious are you, dreams?
Dreams, dreams, oh sweet dreams.

Work

I applied for a job today.
The sign read, "Hiring now."
I entered the building
And told the desk clerk
I want to work right away.

Instead of saying "You can start today,"
The receptionist gave me an application.
"You must first complete this form.
Then return it, and someone will contact you."
However, I want to work right away.

I completed and returned the form.
The clerk then gave me a date for an interview.
I went home and waited.
I received a call to come in for an interview.
I still want to work right away.

After the interview, I was told I had to wait again
Because there were other applicants
Waiting for an interview.
"Again, someone will contact you."
However, I want work right away.

I waited, waited, and waited.
Still I want to work right away.
If a sign read "Hiring now,"
Run away in the opposite direction,
Because to me, "hiring now" means "not now or never."

Therefore, what does "hiring now" really mean?
I want to work right away.

Hugs

Hugs can make you feel secure.
Hugs can make you feel loved.
Hugs can make you feel hopeful.
Hugs can make you feel happy.

Hugs can be a comforter.
Hugs can be encouraging.
Hugs can ease the pain.
Hugs can brighten your day.

Hugs, however, can be deceiving.
Beware of half-arm hugs,
Standoff hugs,
Moreover, especially full-arm hugs with a smile.

Hugs, hugs, how can we judge you?

Friends

When time of great you are here
The days are long and fun, you are by my side
Long hard and weary nights, you are here
You are my friend

The joy of celebrations and promotions, you congratulate me
After a long way of traveling, you let me rest on your shoulder
Lightheaded and dizzy, you stay with me
You are my friend

When the labor gets hard to bear, you help me
During hopeless and downhearted time, you encourage me
The burden of problems and despair, you give me hope
You are my friend

No one to talk with or hear me, you listen to me
All alone and lonely nights, you are there
Stormy weather and rainy days, you calm me
You are my friend

When times of pain and sorrow, you hold my hand
The loss of loved ones and falling tears, you comfort me
When all seems lost, you stand with me
You are my friend

Thank you, God, you are my friend

Ambitious

You were always on the go
Never looking back
Nothing seems to get in your way
Ambitious that was you

Tough, swift, and hardworking
Nothing seems to stop you
Knocked down and tossed to the side
Ambitious that was you

Denied and prosecuted
Broken and lost
Stressed out and abandoned
Ambitious that was you

You built a future and made it big
Ambitious that way you

The Air in My Lungs

The way you make me feel
Gives me a breath of fresh air
I engulf the clean and crispy breeze you bring
You are the air in my lungs

The laughter you have
Brightens my night to day
That fills my lung with love
You are the air in my lungs

You are as necessary in my life
As breathing air is to survive
The joy you give me is like oxygen
You are the air in my lungs

The strong affection of love
That you bring is a profound emotion
You are the best thing that ever happened to me
You are the air in my lungs
You are the air in my lungs

About the Author

Frances J. Hill was born in a small town in Alabama called Castleberry. She was the fourth child born to David Peters Sr. and Levornia L. Peters. She graduated from Conecuh County High School in 1976. She married Eddie J. Watkins, and they had two children, Eddie Jermaine Watkins Sr. and Jamie Franchesca C. Watkins. They have three grandchildren: Eddie Jermaine Watkins Jr., La'Brina Franchesca N. Beasley, and Alaya G. Julia Wallace.

She worked at Vanity Fair Mills, in Monroeville, Alabama, for seventeen years before she decided that was not her career for the rest of her life. Then she enrolled at Patrick Henry Jr. College in Monroeville, Alabama, which is presently called Coastal Community College. She graduated with an associate's degree. She later attended and graduated from Auburn University of Montgomery with a bachelor's and master's degree in education, after which she furthered her education by attending and graduating with an education specialist degree from Alabama State University in Montgomery, Alabama.

She was an educator for twenty years. She taught at Thurgood Marshall Middle School in Evergreen, Alabama, where Mrs. Geneva S. Lyons was her principal. She received two Hank Sanders Grants, one for science and one for reading. She was honored in the Who's Who among America's Teachers in 2003–2004 and 2004–2005. She was a math coach, girls' basketball coach, taught reading, math, and science; wrote two articles in Mid-South Educational Research Association and the University of North Florida.

She is a retired educator who wanted to continue with her dreams. She always wanted to be a writer. She loves reading, working with children, and especially writing poetry. She wants to encourage her children, grandchildren, and students that it is never too late to follow their dreams. Always remember to put God first, and he will see you through.

CPSIA information can be obtained
at www.ICGtesting.com
Printed in the USA
LVHW031203100221
678885LV00004BA/807